Heal Gorgeous: Wisdom Knows the Way

Copyright 2023
Chistell Publishing
https://www.chistell.com
First Printing, April 2023

Published by: Chistell Publishing
                 7235 Aventine Way, Suite #201
                 Chattanooga, TN 37421

Author: Denise Turney
ISBN: 979-8-9856651-3-0

Dedication

For my son.

I love you, Gregory –

Table of Contents

Chapter 1 – Listen

What a Part of Your Knows

Two Ways

Did You Hear It?

Chapter 2 – Self Concept

Self-Creation

Wondering Begats Wandering

Futile Searching

Lifetime

Chapter 3 – Middle Ground

A Losing Bargain

One Way or Another

Not a Safe Place

Chapter 4 – Don't Harness Your Power

Chase Your Dreams

Achieve Your Dreams

What Success Teaches

Chapter 5 – Trust the Process

    You've Heard This Before

    Where You Are, Where You're Going

    Persist

Chapter 6 – Awakening

    Learning Everyday

    Starting to Notice What's Happening

    You Are the Prize

Chapter 7 – Awareness

    In the Stillness

    Pay Attention

    Everywhere you go (you are there)

Chapter 8 – What You Love

    Pursuits Take Time

    Where Is Your Energy Going

    Living With Certainty

Chapter 9 – Preparing for Success

Building a Solid Foundation

Your Attraction to Guilt

Success in an Ever-Changing World

Your Inner Champion (supporting yourself thru cheers and boos)

Chapter 10 – Projecting Your Life

What Is Projection

What Do You See Within?

Change Is an Inside Job

Your Thoughts Matter

Chapter 11 – Waking Up

Perceiving Differently

Off Brain Auto-Pilot

Honest Living

Extending Love

Your True, Original Self

"To listen is to learn."

Chapter 1 – Listen

The real world is rumored to be a place of wonder, brilliance, abstract beauty and glory, but you have to listen to tap into it. In this regard, relating to the world is akin to adjusting to the shifts inherent in a passionate love affair. Refuse to listen to your lover and the relationship sours, melts like a candle left too long in a fire.

Paying attention is the core of listening. When you listen, you focus on a sound, a feeling, a vibration or an activity, a behavior or event that is happening. You don't hide or repress or demand that others act as if what is happening is not occurring. You listen.

Cognitive abilities, natural senses and emotions are involved in the act of listening. So too are memories, an ocean of recollections that can cloud and skew what is being shared.

To listen, you need to be alert. There needs to be a *willingness* to pay attention. No way around it. You must care about what is being shared to listen.

The American College of Healthcare and Technology shares that, "Listening is active, hearing is passive."[1] When something matters enough, piques your interest enough, you start to actively listen.

Therefore, active listening does not require physical hearing. It takes focus and attention. Active listening to the meaningful generates a reward.

Resources:

1. Hearing vs Listening | American College of Healthcare and Technology (ach.edu)

What a Part of You Knows

A part of you knows

the truth

Remember when you were a kid

and you felt like there was a blend of awe and mystery about this world?

You tried to figure out what it was

Life got fast

Your days became busy

Filled up with school, playing, visiting family and so much more

Busyness

You stopped feeling like something was ambiguous with this world because you stopped listening to wisdom

Soon – in no time flat

You looked to the world to tell you what it was

To tell you where you were before you came here

To tell you why you are here

Now you don't remember

the truth

You don't even remember what you truly are

But a part of you knows

Two Ways

There are two ways to listen

You hear a loud noise

So loud you can't ignore it, the kind of noise that wakes you,
shakes you – gets in your face

Even if you don't want to

You listen. It's as if you don't have a choice

You hear the sound, doesn't matter if it's grating, irritating,
happy, sad, anxious, shrilling or nauseating

If the noise is loud enough, different enough

What do you do?

You might think about the sound, wondering where it came
from and why you heard it just when you did

Another decision you might make, all because you listened, is
tell other people about the sound

It was loud! It was sharp! It was dull! It was flat! It was a rolling
noise! It was a banging sound! You say, remembering what you
heard so well, you can easily describe it with clarity

What you won't do, at least not upon first hearing it, is ignore the noise. It's like you can't block it out

You listen.

A friend talks to you about a loud emotional experience, a potential, sudden job change, a relationship struggle, birth of a child, a loved one transitioning, an unexpected housing move or a demanding course they're enrolled in

The timing is off

After all, you've just heard this loud noise

It's a sound that still demands your attention

Seemingly making it impossible to listen to anyone or anything else

This noise burdens your concentration

Imprisons your focus, turning you toward worry

As you try to figure the noise out

What was it exactly?

And why did you hear it?

This noise

This loud noise

If only you could forget this noise

Hours and days pass

You're tired more than usual and you tell yourself that you can't explain why

Off to the doctor you go, but before you get there, before you even leave home, you already know that working a job or staying in a relationship you don't love is draining you

It started as a cold, a mild flu or a bout of sleepiness or sleeplessness

It's getting louder, with the growing fatigue, just not loud enough

So, you decide to ignore it, just like you ignored your friend

You don't listen.

Getting out of bed is getting harder. Colleagues and your manager have started telling you that you seem different, less engaged, tired.

Your friend accepted a job promotion and is moving away, making it hard for you to see her the way you two used to hang out one to two weekends a month

She's busy with the relocation, packing, touring new homes six states away

Finally, you're ready to face what's happening to your energy. You're tired of feeling tired

You call your friend

She answers the phone, but she doesn't listen

She hears your voice making a noise, but she can't feel what you're saying

She doesn't understand

Vitamins, fresh filtered water, a new diet – you try them all

Reward is more fatigue

Sitting up in bed after nine hours of sleep feels too heavy, like too much to do

Your friend moving, your energy fading – it seems like loss

The noise is getting loud

Rising in a grating crescendo, demanding your attention, giving you no choice except to

Listen.

Did You Hear It?

Softness in the rise of a morning sun

The slow tilt from dawn to midday to twilight

Pattering rain taping on hills, mountains, valleys and rooftops

Not brisk, sweeping, pouring and pounding

Flowers filling open fields with the wonder of color and
delightful scents

Did you hear it?

Fresh water pumping out of a well

Sweet berries hanging low on trees, low enough to be picked
with ease

Herbs, medicinal plants and teas in the under bush, less than
half a mile from where a tent was pitched

Fish jumping

Reminders of the importance of play

Rhythm a cluster of birds create, their calls, trills and whistles
going out in a majestic song

Did you hear it?

A red fox reposing at your side, sharing her body heat with you
absent request for payment

Feathers blowing gently across your face as you move through a garden

Laughter erupting in children, free of worldly cares

Releasing you from worry and needling concern

Kids playing a game at the street's edge, reminding you of how you once were, free, full of dreams, hopeful

Did you hear it?

Believe. Keep Going. Dream Huge. Laugh.

Love colored posters plastered to train station walls

Walls you have to pass to get to and from work, to and from school, to and from home

Lyrics to a popular song, a melody that warms your heart until you close your eyes and smile, playing on a nearby radio, as if calling out to you

Did you hear it?

Shadow of a spider creating her web inches above your shoulders, trusting her life so near to you

Light from a neighboring room opening the possibility of a good story entering your day

Snowfall casting a quiet calm

Trees swaying, working like a fan, keeping you cool

Fireflies lighting up night skies

Tart cherries making it easier to drift into sleep

Friends stopping by out-of-the-blue

Letters from an old acquaintance arrive in the nick of time

Did you hear it?

Listen

You are loved

Chapter Two – Self Concept

Could you be holding a concept of yourself that you are afraid to lose? What if this concept is your master, telling you what to do, what to feel, what to believe? But is it true? Is this self-made concept who you really are?

Merriam-Webster defines concept as, "something conceived in the mind: thought, notion." Another definition given for concept is, "an abstract or generic idea generalized from particular instances."[1]

Dictionary.com has this to say about "concept". It is "an idea of something formed by mentally combining all its characteristics or particulars; a construct."[2] Clearly, when exploring a concept, it's necessary to examine the thinker.

Resources

1. Concept Definition & Meaning - Merriam-Webster
2. Concept Definition & Meaning | Dictionary.com

Self-Creation

The concept that you created, are creating, yourself is a rather maddening theory

Especially when you consider that you can never add or take enough away to feel like you finally got it right

That you at last created the self you will always love

After countless years, it would seem that the message had become clear

Your real Self, your real true Self, does not need to be recreated, does not need to be improved upon

Living in that Self is the only thing you need do

Yet, you keep searching for more

More ways to feel better about a self that isn't really you

The pain of that labor must be heavy, hard, depressing

To not accept your true God created Self, to search for a self that will never be real, never satisfy

Must hurt

One day you will choose joy and let the pursuit of this other self
go

You will know you are free then

Wondering Begats Wandering

A traveler

Miles beneath her feet

Came to the end of a long, wide road

She wanted to rest

Yet felt compelled to

Keep moving

Deep inside

There was a certainty

Deeper than faith

Still

She wondered about everything

Where she ventured from –

Had it really fulfilled her?

Where she was headed –

Was it exciting . . . safe?

Was she enough?

Did the Creator really love her?

When people were with her, were they happy in her presence?

Friends she had – were they true?

Happiness she felt – would it last?

So much wondering

No wonder she is wandering

Moving about searching for a home

Someplace safe

A place where safety never leaves or diminishes

Perhaps it's in the next relationship

But she thought that before

Maybe it's in the next job or the next piece of currency

That's not new either

All this wondering

Keeps her wandering

Futile Searching

Searching for a self that doesn't exist

Leads to sorrow and discontent

Perhaps it's time to become curious about what's motivating
this constant search for what can never be found

What are you really looking for?

Is it hidden?

Inside of you?

Lifetime

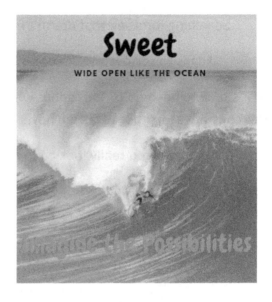

A man

Sitting at a table

By a window

In a café

Saw a folded note

Which he unfolded

It read

"A lifetime equals 90 deep wells. Fill them. Each one."

Ten wells were full of people he met at the café

Sipping herbal teas

Laughing

Telling jokes

Flirting

Embellishing his college years

It was a record high 108 degrees

Scorching hot when

Another note appeared

This one was stuck

In the slit between his door and the wall

"Do more!"

The note read

Not considering the cost

The man took off on a nature quest

Meditating

Praying

Eating wild berries, herbs

Greens and fish

He woke in a library

At the edge of a forest

"Have fun!"

Read a note taped to the library door

The trip into a faraway city

A place bustling with people, noise, cars

Theaters, restaurants, houses, museums, mountains

Flatlands, beaches, shops and gardens

Took 20 whole years

He met a woman, the

Kind of woman that made a man happy to

Wake in the morning but want

To stay in bed all day

and explored the art of romance

Days flowed with wonder, aimless curiosity

Laughter, peace, excitement and calm

Two lovers became six

Time hurried

The wells filled up

Graying hair and a body that could

No longer bend like the curve

In a spoon

Found the man

Sitting

Into long, slow days

Six became two again

Kids growing up fast

She'd been gone for ten minutes

But he didn't remember his wife leaving

Her love warmed him like

The fires

He'd sat by out in nature

When he saw her

Sitting in the chair

His gaze caught a note

Hanging out of her skirt pocket

Ends flat as the middle

"I remember you even now"

The note read

He sat

Note in hand

Like he'd sat at the table

By the window

At the café

Except

This time

He was greeted

With the sweetest berries

Fresh like morning dew

Splendid stories he'd read at the library

Laughter from the theater

Coolness of ocean waves

Brushing against his skin

Hawaii's Pacific Ocean

Surfer's paradise

Babies breath

Playful cooing

Races across the backyard

Showers beneath a waterfall

Kicking at soccer balls with friends

Naps on the sofa

While

Jazz plays softly

On the radio

The last well

Filling up

With the sweetest memories

He'd taken the time to make

Chapter 3 – Middle Ground

At first glance, middle ground looks to be the core of civility. In this world of contrast, that may well be the case.

However, middle ground demands concessions, compromise. If you're aiming for truth, there is no middle ground. The truth is whole, complete. It is not open to compromise, concessions or change.

Could the belief in "middle ground" hint at another proof that the mind that makes an unkind world, invest in a cruel delusion, is operating on the opposite spectrum of truth? But why?

Why invest in such folly and so passionately? If a part of you dwells in truth, what would you sacrifice (e.g., concessions, compromise) to find the truth?

Why venture upon such a search? Why seek something you already have, something your true Self is part of?

In this world, you are either pursuing truth or seeking a lie. There is no middle ground. You cannot seek truth and a lie simultaneously. You either want truth or a lie.

Seeking truth with conviction and commitment can help lead you home.

A Losing Bargain

A lover seeks a lover

with a gift

the lover believes she does not have

was robbed of, tricked out of

Passion accompanies the gift

Time and again the lover longs for what the other might offer,
can give her, at last making her whole

The promise fills the lover with energy, hope, happiness

It's nearly impossible to contain the emotions that accompany
the promise, the hope of becoming whole

Potential to make his lover whole stirs up strength in the lover,
making him feel as if nothing is missing from him

Hope of fulfillment pushes them together, forces their bodies to
merge, melt with passion, seeking to become one

Shouts of their commitment reach out beyond them, impact
family, friends, everyone they know

Then, one day the lover stops searching for what she believes is
missing in her, hunting for what she believes she was robbed of

A harvest of experience

a myriad of events have passed

Time spent with her lover has made it clear to her that her lover's gift is not enough

She is angry, disillusioned, outraged

She feels robbed, tricked

The lover she sought and gained does not have what she believes she was robbed of

Her lover no longer leaves her feeling fulfilled, as if nothing is missing

She feels cheated by her lover not knowing he had been searching for the same thing she had been searching for

He too thought he'd find what he was searching for in her

They keep their discovery a secret

How cheated it feels to believe you're so close to finally becoming whole only to realize that your lover doesn't have what you are looking for

It's a painful, heart wrenching middle ground full of compromise, concessions and loss

One Way or Another

Singing

Dancing

Bargaining

Selling and buying

Marriage

Making a family

Expanding one's footprint in effort to move into a

More rewarding, pleasurable, comfortable condition

Is one way to attempt to enter reality

a returning to a past that exist outside time

a past present eternity of pure love

Seeing yourself suffering

then thrusting that suffering from yourself onto another

in the form of

Belittling

Ridicule

Violence

Separating

is another way to attempt to enter reality

a returning to a past that exist outside time

a past present eternity of pure love

Then there's stillness

a quiet acceptance of the truth about yourself

An inward road, twisting, turning, climbing, ascending

Sending you deeper

Deeper

Inside truth

Any other way is middle ground

attempts at nothingness

You will get home

Not a Safe Place

Have you ever felt tired, exhausted, absent the energy to take another step, sit up, laugh, cry, do anything?

Perhaps you're working a job, doing volunteer work or in a relationship that leaves you feeling flat

Thoughts of leaving cross your mind, flood your thinking

Yet, you push

Pushing the thoughts away is a pattern you've grown accustomed to

Stay on middle ground

Don't go too far one way or another

Live on middle ground

Avoid upsetting the manager and colleagues at work, team members at the volunteer organization, your beau

Sacrifice your peace under the disguise that doing so will keep those in your life from having to sacrifice what they want

It's not a safe place

You'll never get what you want, live in a place of joy and peace, if you keep forfeiting your joy and peace

Just so you can stay on middle ground

It's not a safe place

Yes. You may have to go it alone when you speak truth, when you choose again, this time going for what is right

But you won't sacrifice your joy, and you'll live in peace

Each time you decide to live off the middle ground, in a loving, peaceful, truth-based way, you'll take a step closer to home, to remembering your real, true Self

The longer you live on middle ground, the more you forget your real, true Self

What you really want

The path to joy and peace

*****

You've seen how it works

After weeks, months, years of sacrificing for another, what they want becomes your focus, your goal, your pathway

No longer getting still to hear from your Creator, you ask your siblings, colleagues, friends, which way you should go

They don't know, but you turn to them still

It's the price for seeking guidance from an unsafe place

Either way, you'll pay

The illusional price to pay for following your true Self ranges from public disapproval to ridicule to hearing others tell you why you should go a different way, live on middle ground

Yet, following your true Self is *really* not a price. It's

More a reward disguised as temporary loss

Stay on the path and see if you don't start to feel alive, eager to create new, exciting experiences

See if

Confidence in love rises

See if

Hope for better experiences increases

See if

Trust in truth gets stronger

See if

Clarity about which way you should go, regardless of what is happening to and around you, sharpens

Unlike the middle ground

Now you are in a safe place

Chapter 4 – Don't Harness Your Power for Good

A harness is used to put something under another's control. It's a device used to keep something from doing too much of what it wants, from being independent, an aim some refer to as "stubbornness".

If a hidden, unhealed part of your mind gets the keys and decides to harness your power, you could feel a need to shrink. You could also feel small, of little importance, insignificant and incomplete.

Let that happen and you could go months or years feeling like something is missing, searching for this seemingly "missing" part in other people, work, patterns or chemicals. The most unfortunate effect could happen if you start to really believe that you are inadequate, simply not enough.

Today, consider removing the harness. Free yourself as you decide to do good.

Chase Your Dreams

Remember when you were a kid?

Back then, did you hear a dream?

Maybe the dream told you that you could fly to outer space, be a champion race car driver, discover a cure for a disease, create new music, be a masterful architect or an amazing educator

Did excitement erupt inside you when the dream was revealed to you?

Or did you tell yourself that the dream was too big, made for someone better, stronger, financially wealthier, more important than you?

What did it feel like as you stepped inside the dream, let yourself submerge beneath the dream's tremendous possibilities?

Did you feel alive, like fulfilling the dream is what you came here for?

Could you revisit the dream, recall it in great clarity, with tremendous emotion?

Would you?

Or would you try to convince yourself that it's too late, time to chase your dreams has passed you by?

How does it feel watching other people chase and fulfill their dreams?

Do you feel a conviction, a knowing that, except for your reluctance not to give your life over to fear, you too could soar?

You're reading this now

What are you waiting for, Gorgeous?

Go fulfill that dream!

Wake up and Live

Achieve Your Dreams

It's not enough to chase a dream, you have to fulfill the dream

Put your heart into what you are trying to do

Stir up your courage, facing fears about potential failure, setbacks and disappointments

Seek out and talk to others who are doing what you want to do, asking them what the start, middle and endings of the dream are like

Get started, watching a film or reading books related to your dream

Attend events people with a dream like yours attend

Talk to these people, building rewarding relationships, networks that work like bridges from where you are to where you want to be

Study your dream, observe it with great curiosity

Then, get started, buying supplies, learning, developing and sharpening your craft

If your dream is to be a business, social or community leader, start leading teams, even while you're a kid

It's never too early or too late to pursue your dreams

The sooner you get started, the more you learn

The longer you could enjoy the fruits of your dream fulfillment, not to mention having time and energy to chase and achieve more dreams

Chasing and achieving your dreams teaches you a lot

About yourself and the world

Achieving your dreams changes your perceptions

Makes you see life anew

Restores your confidence

Guides you toward what really matters, especially as you achieve your dreams and discover that, by itself, dream fulfillment is not enough

But you'll never learn this if you don't chase and achieve your dreams

Instead, you'll spend your time in this world guessing at how things could be, might have been

Why live that way when you don't have to?

Find out for sure, then move on to the next phase of learning

Let yourself be pointed to more truth

That guidance may not come until after you achieve your dreams, as dream fulfillment might be part of the process

So, what are you waiting on?

Why delay the awakening?

Go achieve your dreams

There's more awaiting after you take that step

But first, you have to achieve your dreams

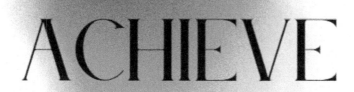

What Success Teaches

Achieve a goal, complete a project or face a fear then attain something you've wanted and it feels like the universe opens up for you

The small space you had been living in expands

Before you know it, you're envisioning yourself doing greater things

You're starting to believe

Small things that once annoyed you, no longer needle you

It's as if you're starting to see what really matters

Distractions don't rob your focus the way they formerly did

Another thing that happens as you move from success to success is you start to see that getting what you want, what you really think you want, the type of wanting that keeps you up at night, doesn't keep you in a state of joy forever

You would never start to see this if you didn't start chasing your dreams and gain the success that you long for

Gone are the beliefs that it's failure that is the great teacher

Thanks to the success you're experiencing, you're learning a lot – not from failure, but from success

Keep succeeding

There's a lot to learn

Chapter 5 - Trust the Process

Look back over your life and you may see that you are in process. You've never stayed in the same place internally. Emotions and thoughts that you've experienced change.

If only you could see what was coming. Then, it might be easier to see what is happening, that you are in process. But life in this world doesn't come with the type of roadmap that outlines where you are, where you're going and all the steps that you need to take to get to your destination.

In this world, you have to trust the process. That means that you have to love yourself enough to believe that what's guiding the process can only love you.

You have to love yourself to the point that you cannot concept of anyone or anything being capable of doing anything other than loving you. That's the power of truly loving yourself, not in a false way like narcissism, but in truth.

Trusting the process becomes easier then. You also find peace and joy as you take each step in the process.

You've Heard This Before

Sixty years into a dream, a woman

A knee jabbing her with pain

Traveled to an ocean's edge to

Consult a sage

"I knew you would come."

She listened to the sage say

Blustering wind forced her forward

Closer to the sage

"Love yourself if you want to experience continual joy and peace."

The sage told her

"Treat yourself the way you want other people to treat you.

Care for yourself the same as you care for those you love

There's a power in loving yourself, a power you can't gain from doing anything else

You've heard this before, but are you listening?

Have you really and fully taking the message in?

Are you patient with yourself, giving yourself space to learn and awaken?

Do you keep reminding yourself about mistakes you made or do you receive the lesson from the error and move on, progressing and advancing?

The way you perceive or think about yourself matters

Driving everything you do and think you can do

Empowering dreams or fueling fears

You've heard this before, but are you listening?"

Gone from the sage and

At first sight of her home

The woman found her thoughts returning to, filling up with the sage, making her feel like a deep well

Her hands shook when

She turned the key to her home and

Peered inside the looking glass

Her hands went down her face

Like water going down a vine

Her face

Her face

It looked like the sage's

Only younger

Where You Are, Where You're Going

Before you can get to where you want to be, it's important to know where you are right now.

It takes honesty (not cruelty) to acknowledge where you are.

This isn't where you wish you were. It's where you actually are at this instant.

Do you wake each morning feeling hope, appreciation, anger, fear, excitement, anxiety, love, despair or motivation?

What do you do each morning, afternoon and evening?

Your patterns and routines could be keeping you where you are. Not changing your patterns and routines could be a sign that you are afraid to make progress, to leave where you are, to actually get to where you want to be.

Do you practice awareness and take time to watch what you are thinking, feeling and doing each day or do you live on default, as if your life doesn't really matter?

Are you stepping back and simply watching where your life goes, where you end up, as if you have no say in what happens to you?

It may help to pull out a roadmap.

Look at landmarks, showcasing where you are.

Then look at landmarks for places where you could go that are outlined on the roadmap.

What routes can you take to get from point A to point B?

Anything exciting along the way that you could stop and explore, making the path that much more rewarding?

You've got it!

Have fun along the way.

Enjoy learning, exploring, playing and growing and awakening as you continue to move forward.

Believe it or not, it's what happens to you as you progress, step-by-step, toward your destination that makes being where you are beautiful.

Even if it's tempting, don't rush.

After all, it will be over before you know it.

Enjoy each step that you take, each person and living being you meet.

Do it sincerely, loving yourself no matter what, and you might start enjoying the journey as much as the idea of living where you're going.

That's when you start to see the wonder of life, the wonder of bringing amazing-wonderful you to the space that you're occupying.

If that space could speak, it might sing or shout, "Yes!"

Just because you are there.

Persist

Regardless of what you want to achieve or experience, persist if you want what has been developing in your mind to show up in the perceptual world.

Persist to shift the image, the idea, the experience from deep within your mind to the level of mind that sees and interacts with other sights, people, animals, plants and visible life in this world.

This is not to say that the work will be easy. You may have to push, be resilient and tenacious.

What you won't be able to do is give up, not if you want to bring the experience into this world.

The first thing you try to bring from an idea in your mind into an actual, touchable experience in this world might not work.

Keep going.

Keep trying.

Ask your subconscious for more ideas on what you can do to shift the idea from your mind to the world.

Realize that the shift will bring changes into your life.

Do your homework.

Make sure that you are ready to merge the changes that the shift brings into your life.

Start preparing for the changes.

Show yourself that you can adapt to the changes without hurting yourself, while loving yourself more and more.

This single act might reduce or eliminate any fear that a part of you has about the shift.

When you consider how committed the brain is to keep you safe and to help you survive, the importance of proving to yourself that you'll stay safe after the shift occurs could be a huge key to you opening up and allowing the shift to happen.

So, love yourself and show yourself that you will always love you and accept that the Creator keeps you safe -- and persist.

Get curious about what it's going to take to bring the shift about.

Get so curious that you become passionate about trying different strategies, different ways of approaching what it is you want to do, what you know you must do.

Until the door opens

Chapter 6 – Awakening

Every experience, every person you meet, every passion and idea you pursue can be used toward your awakening, aid in renewing your mind. The key is to pay attention to what seems to be happening to and around you.

Pay attention.

Try not to attach meaning to what you see, hear and feel. If your interpretations and judgments are in error, you could set yourself on the wrong path, believing what is not true.

Accepting that you don't know everything is an excellent way to allow new information, truth, to surface from deep within your true Self. Stay open while you practice awareness.

Allow new ideas to surface. You might even find it helpful to do parts work as you continue renewing your mind and open to awakening to your One, True Self. It's a day-by-day quest, an ongoing process with eternal rewards.

Learning Everyday

"Let's pause and catch our breath," one friend said to another.

Below them were miles of rugged mountainside.

A day ago, one friend had fallen

Nearly breaking an arm

A purplish bruise on the thigh like

Risen patch quilt

It hurt

Remembrance of a hard lesson

Both friends were more careful now

"Don't let it get you down," one friend said to the other.

"These things happen, and we will continue."

Sorrow settled into the face of the friend who had fallen.

The other friend pitched a tent.

"It's all mountain, don't you see?" The friend said, hammering a
tent peg into the ground.

"It's all a lesson. Chin up. You fell, but you are not a fall."

The friend with sorrow in the face listened,

Eager to be nudged away from sorrow.

Another tent peg went inch-by-inch into the ground

"Learning is part of life in this world," the friend said, tossing thick plastic across the ground before raising the tent with a silver pole.

"The more you learn, the more you can take on.

When you think about it, you'll see that trust is part of learning, part of good living. It's like climbing this mountain. The more we learn, the more we trust, just like the higher up this mountain we go, the more we trust that we can keep climbing."

Massaging the bruise, the friend gave a nod then started splitting dry firewood.

Merely feet away and busy constructing the portable stove's chimney pipe, the other friend said, "The more room you give yourself to explore, try new things, the bigger the world gets. We see that from up here. Look around. We can see it even now."

"Finished with the chimney?" the friend with sorrow in the face asked.

"Almost."

They spent the next several minutes breathing in an awkward silence, a silence that thickened the space between them.

"Steer clear of thinking that a fall will repeat. What happened yesterday may never happen again. We have to keep opening up to life, living larger, learning more and climbing. It's what we love to do, right?"

"Yes," the friend who had fallen admitted.

"The fear you're feeling will go away. When you have stopped being afraid of falling, take a smart risk. Take a chance that will reward you. After your thigh mends, let's take a swim in a river. What do you say?"

"Sure. After my thigh mends."

"Where do you think you will go after we reach the summit and the plane comes to fly us home?"

"Don't know," the friend shrugged. "Someplace fun, somewhere new and different. That's for sure."

"Good. Keep exploring. Keep trying new things, so you can keep learning. It's part of the climb."

Starting to Notice What's Happening

The sooner you notice what's happening, the sooner you can "choose again" and make a change that turns you in the direction you truly want to move in

Another blessing that you gain is beginning to notice the similarities between what is happening within and around you

Soon you may learn what happens that's meant to lead you forward vs. what happens that's meant to take you backwards or keep you where you are

If you don't notice what's happening, years could pass before you start to notice which direction your experiences might be moving you in

Part of living in this world is paying attention, noticing what's happening

Instead of judging what is happening, simply observe what happens around you

If you notice your experiences repeating, moving in a circle even if it's a wide circle that takes three to four years to loop, find an experience that you can easily start to insert change into

Again, pay attention

Notice what happens after you insert change into the loop

Keep at it, being willing to witness and adjust to new changes that you insert into your life

These insertions allow you to start living consciously, taking responsibility for your life

Remember

If you don't pay attention

You won't notice what's happening

Life, for you, may appear to occur

Seemingly without any input or decisions from you

That's why life might feel unfair

It's as if events are just happening to you without any input from you

Who wouldn't feel as if they were being treated unfairly, as if their life was being thrust upon them absent any foreknowledge, seemingly absent a single clue about what could occur in their life if they made certain decisions

You've got it!

Noticing what happens to and around you is a great way to start to see the hidden parts of your mind that are deciding and making your experiences

Do this and

An odd thing will occur

You'll start to feel empowered

Even if it's in tiptoe steps, courage to choose again, making better decisions, trying new things

Prepare yourself

A new life might be beginning for you

You Are the Prize

Prize for all your efforts, all your stillness, paying attention and better decision making is the real YOU

Coming into contact with your real True Self is the reward for all your efforts, be they great in your perception or be they small

And what a reward

To finally see your God given, God created Self

To stop finding anything to judge

To decide to love and only love

Imagine completely changing the way you see once and for all

Finally

Not finding a spot when you look at Yourself

When you finally see Yourself again

Really see Yourself in truth

It's a wonderful homecoming

What you've been striving for

Gone is the fear that once held you hostage

Thumping you and jabbing you with accusations, calling you weak, insignificant and incapable of living a good life, thriving and soaring forever

Can you catch a hint of the difference between the you that you have spent years thinking you are and the real, True YOU?

All the work that you do to journey to your one true Self will reduce the shock that you could feel when you finally SEE what you truly are

So, keep doing the internal work.

Keep seeing yourself as worth the stillness, the curiosity and the questioning and more that helps to lead you home

Following Christ and trusting

You'll soon remember how marvelously You are created when you awaken to your one true Self

Chapter 7 – Awareness

Oddly, fear, an illusion, is a state that peaks our awareness. That could be a reason why we might be attracted to fear. When we feel fear, we sharpen. We really pay attention. We're very aware.

Everything we see and hear becomes important. Our brain's amygdala region is activated when we experience fear. During this state, our brain is ready to respond to stimuli, be that stimuli a sight, a sound or a feeling, as in someone bumping us.

The state of awareness that fear puts us in can seem to come with benefits, at least at the onset. But, as you may have noticed, in this world, life is built with patterns and routines.

Before you know it, and as if the effects of fear were a drug, you're remembering events that caused you to feel afraid. That or you create stories, catastrophize opportunities and promise yourself that life won't get better, all so you can re-enter the pattern and routine of fear.

It's a bad-bad habit.

Fortunately, there's another way to feel alert, focused and like you're living with clarity. You can get there by practicing awareness.

It's as simple as consciously choosing to be where you are, focusing on what you're doing right now. This state exists outside the realm of daydreaming and fantasy.

Start small, practicing awareness for one minute then two minutes, moving up to five minutes. Allow the beneficial practice to become a routine, a rewarding add to your life.

Pay attention to what comes into your awareness. And know that when you focus on one thing, you are choosing not to focus on countless other things.

Therefore, as you practice awareness, pay attention to how you feel. If you notice that your thoughts are often negative or that you often expect unwanted experiences to come to you, shift your focus and become aware of the good within you. Watch the changes that come from that single new decision.

In The Stillness

Stillness is great ground to practice awareness

In stillness, you aren't distracted

You're focused, sure and confident

There's no need to work or to feel alright about yourself

Incorporate getting still into your day, maybe each hour, and you may find it easier to connect with your true Self

Let that happen and higher levels of guidance can bubble up to you fast, without effort

All because you entered stillness

Scriptures speak about stillness, noting that it is a way to remember our Creator

Yet, this boundless reward faces a seemingly ever present temptation

What is that temptation?

The temptation to fill days with action, anything to keep from entering stillness

How do your mornings start?

Can you see yourself rushing to the gym, work desk, smartphone, kitchen or to your children's bedrooms (if you're a parent)? If not rushing there, are you rushing someplace else?

Look back

Are you in the habit of rushing away from stillness as soon as you awaken?

A hectic schedule might even find you feeling as if you're earning your keep, being super productive and are doing what all good people do – cramming your days with activity

Years pass and you haven't connected with your true Self

Price of that is you're feeling sluggish, flat or empty, definitely not the way you were created to feel

Off to the doctor you rush, eager to discover why you're not feeling your optimal best

Tests are run

You might even demand a prescription, chemicals which could push your body into an out-of-balance condition

Years could pass before you consider that the cure could be entering stillness, not once, not just during an emergency, but each and every day

If you're accustomed to running here and there, if that's how you feel valuable and worthy to participate in another person's life, be that at work, in the community or at home, be patient as you start to enter stillness

Also, understand that many rewards associated with stillness show up on the inside

You might not see much change in the external world, but you should definitely experience shifts in your internal world

Pay Attention

Paying attention opens the door for you to notice what is happening

When you pay attention, you can make smart choices

You'll see that you don't have to pretend

Nor will you have to live in a fantasy

You can live with the assurance that you will be guided in the right way

But you have to pay attention

You have to pay attention to emotions as they can serve as guides, similar to how a magnet comes with an energetic pull, guiding you in a specific direction

Gone is the feeling that you're floating, simply drifting here and there

It's more than having a purpose or being aware of what you came into this world to do

It's clear direction, the type of direction that can reduce errors that you make, lower second guessing and fill you with confidence and reassurance

Turn away from the guidance, not once, but again and again and you should know that a part of you doesn't want the guidance

A part of you wants to stay where you are, may even want to experience being lost repeatedly, as if innocent of the chaos it's causing, taking delight in watching you spin and turn and try to figure things out

This is a time for trust

Should you continue to go around in circles, pretending as if you don't know what's happening and can't stop yourself, be loving but firm with yourself

Act with conviction and love

Do what you know is the right thing to do

Pay attention

Pay attention to what's happening to and around you

Don't try to figure things out

Simply pay attention, living free of past perceptions while being wise

Life in this world is often a step-by-step or an experience-by-experience process

Release the pull to see the end from where you are

Resist the pull to figure your entire life out

For now, just pay attention

Notice emotional impulses, including the direction that these emotional impulses lead you in

It's through paying attention that you can begin to connect experiences, dreams, intuition, answers to prayer and other guidance forms, pointing you in the direction you should go

Everywhere You Go (You Are There)

Have you ever been so frustrated with yourself that you felt you would feel happier if you could switch lives with someone else, someone who seems happier than you do "to you"

Someone who seems to always be smiling (even though you don't see the person all the time)

Someone with a rich, healthy, robust laugh, the kind of laugh that is contagious, pulling other people in, seemingly causing them to laugh too, joining in the merriment and light-heartedness

Someone people always speak fondly of, complimenting the person, eager to share how wonderful they perceive the person as being

You compare and contrast yourself with this person and keep deciding that you come up lacking

If only you could be more like this beloved person

If only you could stop being you for awhile

Yet, despite your efforts

Everywhere you go, there you are

Although you could continue to wish that you were someone else, finding and pointing out your faults to yourself, if only in your mind

As much of a habit this could become

This is the type of habit that will only bring pain

Because wherever you go, you are there, you have to start looking for and looking at the light within you

You have to start seeing your own inner brilliance, the brilliance that links you to your Creator

The light that comes from your Creator, blending into and with you

You have to learn to love yourself

Be gentle with yourself

Chapter 8 – What You Love

Regardless of what you believe, regardless of what you have experienced, regardless of the depth of pain you might have felt, there is something that you love. Consider the people in your life, your children, siblings, friends or spouse.

Or maybe there's something that you absolutely love to do. Perhaps you love designing houses or racing cars or maybe you love to design fashions and sew. Science, technology and education might be what causes you to feel loved and embraced by love. Then, it might be the arts, singing, dancing, writing, acting that you love.

Whatever it is, this thing ignites a brilliant spark within you each time you engage in it. If it's a person, you feel an overwhelm of love when you are in their presence.

This spark is proof that love has power. Because of this power, what you love will change your life. What you love will change the "you" that you identify as in this world.

Pursuits Take Time

Two sisters sat across from each other

In a small photo booth

The kind of photo booth found in some malls

The younger sister placed a hand on the older sister's shoulder, "This picture we're about to take is meant to earmark a huge part of our history."

At first the older sister smiled, then she laughed, shook her head and frowned.

"Oh, Sister," the younger woman said. "Pursuing a passion does not, by itself, set up a scenario that finds us creating an environment that helps us earn a full income doing what we love. This type of pursuit, although rich with appreciation, may take time."

"It's been decades since I painted my first piece of art. Not a few days or weeks, but decades," the older sister sighed.

"Smile when we look into that camera, because everything is about to change."

Rolling her eyes up toward the booth ceiling, the older sister was quick. "You've always been hopeful."

"I am hopeful. You don't see it, but your dream is going to come true. It may take time because a part of you, perhaps a part you keep hidden out of conscious awareness, doesn't believe in what you are trying to do."

The older sister swatted the air, as if pushing her younger sister's words aside.

"That or a hidden part of you might fear changes that will show up in your life if you reach your goal. I know you think you're ready, but maybe a part of you isn't. Although, to your conscious, that part seems not to exist, it's active, planning, preparing and stopping events from happening to you, from popping up in your awareness as much as your conscious mind is busy making preparations and mapping out paths to your goal."

Laughing until her voice caught in her throat and she snorted, the older sister leaned forward. "I've tried everything, and you know it. Art festivals, street vendors, mall popup booths, craft shows, websites – you name it. I've done it."

"If you want to shorten the time it takes to reach your goal, get to know yourself. Now. Now," she continued, raising her hand. "Study your ego and how it operates. Even more, get to know your true Self."

Rocking her head from side to side, the older sister shouted, "No."

Passersby, shopping bag handles weighing on their palms, looked toward the booth. None stopped, only looking, satisfying their curiosity about what they'd heard.

The older sister's reluctance emboldened the younger sister. "Don't give up. You've heard it before. Repetition doesn't make it untrue. Success is about the journey to who you really are."

Peering at her sister, she continued, "Don't stop just because your paintings haven't taken off yet. I know it seems far away, but if you keep going and take the right actions, each action will bring you closer to where you want to be."

"Right actions? Right actions!" the older sister laughed. "There's nothing I haven't done in pursuit of this dream." She shook her head. "Wish I hadn't been told how good my artwork was when we were kids. The encouragement pushed me down this road. I could be doing something else right now."

"You are doing something else. You're working full-time as a realtor. But you can't give up on your dream."

"Why?"

"It's connected to something much deeper. What you *really want* is to live from your One True Self. You must be patient as you move through internal mental roadblocks."

The older sister leaned back, "Roadblocks?"

"You've felt afraid before, haven't you?"

"Let's not state the obvious."

"Fear can show up as disbelief, not believing that you could live the life you want in this world. Disbelief that you could paint artwork that is tagged with high value, prices that net you millions."

She shrugged, "I know you don't want to hear this, but the time it takes to receive what you want is up to you."

They sat across from each other, looking at each other.

Kids ran across the mall floor, close to the booth, their feet creating a thunderous noise, their voices going up in laughter and song.

"How ready are you?" the younger sister asked. "How much do you want what you say you want?"

The older sister's mouth swung open, but the younger sister was quicker. "How ready are you to face facts about your ego, the illusionary identity you believe is the real you? If you don't get to know yourself, you'll just run from one wish to another."

"I don't want the world," the older sister said. "I just want to earn enough from my paintings to pay my bills, travel and have a fun, amazing life."

"Yes," the younger sister nodded. "Like you said, you've tried so much else. It's time to take the inner journey. Find out what you've been telling yourself. Besides, even if your paintings take off and you don't take the inner journey, you'll merely pursue awards, money, compliments, applause, houses or relationships. You gain these wants only to still feel as if something is missing, as if there is something else that you must pursue."

"You've never done what I'm trying to do. You don't paint. You don't hustle art. I'm telling you, I've tried everything. Can't count how much money I've spent on marketing and advertising."

It was as if the younger sister didn't hear her. She didn't back off. "Thinking that the solution is outside you, off you go in pursuit of another goal, a different dream."

"Listen, Sister," she said. "You could shortcut this process by reading biographies and autobiographies, seeing how other people chased after one dream or goal, only to fulfill that dream and feel an emptiness, then an urge to pursue another goal, all while ignoring the inner longing to journey back to their One True Self."

"Something gave me this gift. Something moved me toward painting when I was a kid. It's not like I just picked this passion out of thin air," the older sister balked.

"That's what I'm getting at. You're right. Your gift and your dream are a ticket to something better. Your dream is so big that you won't get it if you don't take this inner journey."

The older sister stood to leave.

"Please don't," the younger sister pleaded. "Not only does it take time to get what you're pursuing out here in the world. These outer pursuits will go on and on until, in an instant, you realize that the experience you really, truly want is to awaken to the real YOU."

Be
Patient
with yourself

Keep Going

Where Is Your Energy Going?

Energy moves

Dances

Speeds up

Slows down

Takes on form

Releases form

Continues

Peculiar how thoughts direct energy

Influence energy

Moving it this way or that way

Can you feel it?

Joy dancing inside of you

Sorrow and regret and guilt slowing you down

Can you feel it?

Hope igniting the light within

Can you feel it?

Can you feel which way your energy is going?

Are you feeling more

Joy, Peace and Love

There's no room for trades

Swapping out your peace for a relationship with someone who belittles you, tells you lies, makes you feel small and insignificant, like you are something other than your

One True Self

As if this person made you, like they were a makeshift god

Swap outs won't work

Why?

They don't lead you to joy

They won't even make you feel happiness

Sounds simple

But it takes trial and error to learn this

Until you learn this, your energy will shift, focusing here and there

Moving seemingly with abandon

No focus

Just shifting

Until you tire of this dance, this

Aimless, pointless movement

And start to allow your thoughts to be

Directed by the light within

More Peace

Improved Clarity

Real Joy

Boundless Love

Capture your attention

Become your focus

The way your energy turns

Moves

Flows

Living With Certainty

There is a peace in certainty, a sweet peace

That transcends all efforts to use loud voice, threats and bravado in efforts to be courageous

Efforts that fail because you really aren't certain

You aren't certain of your true worth

You don't even remember what you really are

That lack of knowing creates constant uncertainty

Trying new and different jobs, relationships, routines and hobbies proves not to be the cure despite how many times you try

Even if it takes you a long time to notice that you're living with this constant uncertainty, notice it you eventually will

First, you might blame your job, a long commute, colleagues, your parents, siblings, neighbors, where you live, how much money is in your bank account

Anything except what you keep telling yourself

About you

If this sounds odd, you might be hiding your inner thoughts and inner talk from your consciousness

No wonder you keep thinking that someone or something outside of you, other than you, is creating the uncertainty

Fortunately, after awhile this constant uncertainty will try to nag at you, nipping at your emotions and the self-identity you have made for yourself

The way you see yourself, what you tell others you are

Is the self-identity you created for yourself, piecing together personality, hobbies, routines, beliefs and preferences and dislikes based on your perceptions of experiences you have had since you entered this world

Keeping you in a state of eternal peace and joy?

Pay attention to how you think of yourself, how you describe yourself to others

This, again, is part of the self-identity that you have made of yourself

Not only do others perceive you this way

More importantly, this is the way that you perceive you

Pay attention to your feelings

Is there a certainty linked to the self-identity that you have made of you?

If so, you're certain about this self-identity, the way you perceive yourself

Let someone ask you to do something that doesn't align with this self-identity, and up comes the feeling of uncertainty

Years of this recurrence and you might start to "hate" the world, fatigue of the constant uncertainty

Not once realizing that you feel the deepest, hardest uncertainty when you are asked to do something that is far away from the self-identity you made

For example, if you see yourself as a race car driver, you might feel uncertainty if you're asked to lead an engineering project even after an engineer offers you sufficient training to be able to ace leading the project

Or you might perceive yourself as a florist, putting together beautiful, colorful bouquets, only to feel intense uncertainty when someone ask you to deliver the keynote speech at a local college

Impactful public speaker may not be part of the self-identity that you made

Hence – uncertainty

Should the world not alter to fit the self-identity that you made, you might pull back, isolate yourself or only allow yourself to be in environments that fit this self-identity.

Smaller and smaller the world starts to feel

Which way out you wonder

Let go of the self-identity that you made

Slowly, instant by instant, day by day

Week by week, month by month

Year by year let this self-identity go

Your One True Self is immeasurably larger than any self an illusion could make of you

You can do more than you can imagine if you release this self-identity

Start releasing the self-identity that you made by taking smart risks, follow through on ideas received from Light

If you do, you might be surprised to be led to training programs that help prepare you for what you are about to do, the type of training that alters the self-identity you made

Allowing courage to deepen within you

Eventually you come to see that you did not and cannot create yourself and you journey back to your

One True Created Self

Chapter 9 – Preparing for Success

Preparing for success is a sure sign that you believe in the good that is about to happen to you, is a sign that you *expect* to achieve a goal. Part of this preparation might include developing a budget to manage your finances after you find yourself dealing with a significant income increase. Planning could also find you speaking with your family about time, travel, speaking engagement, etc. adjustments you need to make to deal with success.

Mentally preparing for changes that could enter your life after you achieve the success you're seeking is another sign that you know, absolutely know, that you are going to succeed. For example, you might make sitting still for two to five minutes a day, spending 45 minutes in nature and gaining plenty of restorative sleep a priority.

Another decision that you might make as you prepare for success is to strengthen your relationships with family and friends, ensuring that you have a strong support system, keeping you from seeking out strangers, people who might be infatuated with you and your success but who don't know you.

Learning about regulated investments, solid investment instruments, marketing resources and beautiful residential neighborhoods (should you want to move) are other ways to prepare for success. So too is creating a disciplined practice of regularly designing new products and services to build sustainable income.

By preparing for success, you can reduce the stress you might have felt if you had been unexpectedly flooded with the immense change success brings. Therefore, preparation could shield you from retreating from wins and empower you to adjust to success in healthy ways.

Also, before the success manifest, simply by preparing for its arrival, you could open up to manifesting success more. Rather than resisting success, you might make room for it.

Building a Solid Foundation

Knowing you are going to live in the success you're pursuing encourages new actions. You will want to build a solid foundation of support that includes family and friends who knew you before success manifested.

Think about the support you will need.

People you can trust, the type of people who won't sell made-up stories about you to tabloids for a hefty price.

People who won't get jealous of your victories regardless of how much success you enjoy.

People who feel worthy and confident and loved without needing to befriend those who are celebrated.

People who fully hold their own, loving living in their True being.

Building a solid foundation *now* can shield you from betrayal, shocking surprises that could cost you huge sums of money, peace of mind and more.

Building a solid foundation helps you to relax as you realize that there is a team of people who are not only ready, but deeply willing, to support your success.

You may not realize the full impact of building a solid foundation *before* you step into the success you want until *after* the success arrives.

However, if you wait until the success is here to start building a solid foundation,

It could be too late.

You might not find anyone whose perception of you hasn't changed, which could put you on the search for distant lands, for people you have never met before.

Believing that, simply because you and these people are strangers, there's something about them you can trust.

This might only be an illusion.

An erroneously perceived, trustworthy friend might actually be a well-dressed, well-rehearsed foe.

A solid foundation can save you from this sorrowful surprise.

Yes! You can live with immeasurable success while being surrounded by people who love you.

It is possible.

Believe tremendous success is coming to you?

Start now to build a solid foundation.

Attraction to Guilt

Attraction to guilt is costing you more than you know

More than you are willing to forfeit

Despite your attraction to guilt

You do want a peace that transcends time

You really do want boundless, timeless, eternal JOY

Yet, a part of you wants to hold onto the past

Rather than to step into a bright NOW

You keep choosing to bring a painful past into your current experiences

Sometimes it can take years of therapy or deep inner-work

To realize that you are attracted to guilt

To see that you keep choosing to hold onto past painful experiences

Bringing them into the NOW

As if these painful experiences are meant to have an eternal impact

On you

When they aren't

When you're ready to let go of guilt

Stop pursuing it

Cease attacking yourself with pain

Then projecting those internal attacks

Onto others

When you're ready to let go of guilt

Start to "really" SEE YOU

Start to "really" SEE other created beings

As they truly are RIGHT NOW

Free of past perceptions, beliefs or past thoughts

Allowing yourself and all those you meet

To have a clean slate

Not one stain, spot or wrinkle from an unforgiven past on them

Getting to the real world where there is no guilt or pain

Might start with imagining

Imagining what it will feel like when you are no longer attracted
to guilt

Imagining what it will feel like when you enter each instant

Brand new

Without feeling impelled to protect yourself

Because you finally realize that the Creator would never allow your One True Self to be harmed

Imagine what it will feel like when you fully forgive yourself for any past perceived mistakes

Imagine what it will feel like when you fully forgive all living beings

Holding no guilt or desire to attack against

Yourself

Success in an Ever-Changing World

You've worked hard for

Years, perhaps decades

Attending networking events, marketing and advertising your products and services

Continuing your education, attending online and offline trainings related to your passion field

Always seeking to deepen what you know

Sharpening your skills

Trying to keep up with people you refer to as your competition

Avoiding falling behind

Striving to get farther and farther away from where you started in the world, be that the projects, a ghetto, upscale community, religious environment or in a home where your parents pushed, cajoled and demanded that you do what they did, only better, or that you do what they always wanted to do but never got up enough courage to

Pursuing success in an ever-changing world

May be working like a barricade

Keeping you from believing that you can rest

Actually rest

Fortunately

You really want what you want

Desire creates persistence

Tenacity

Commitment

In You

However long it takes, you realize your dreams

Obtaining the success you've dreamed and prayed about

The next several years are smooth sailing

It's sweet settling into success

Then, seemingly out of nowhere

Things shift

Marketing strategies are now only pulling in 60% of the orders
they once pulled in

Technologies you need to maintain your current success levels,
the very levels you lived without for decades but have now
become so accustomed to

You feel as if you will suffer if the success evaporates

But things are shifting

Fast

To the point where you wonder

Stress over whether you can keep up

With the changes and still be successful

Fortunately

You really want what you want

So, you pivot

Like a car navigating a slippery road

You don't fight the shifts, the changes

Instead, you keep your focus

The goal you've been pursuing is still the same

It's the path to the goal that you're willing to alter, keeping healthy boundaries in play

Why?

The goal is what's important to you

You're also starting to learn that success in an ever-changing world does not come with permanence

Although you don't know when the next shift will come

Of this you are now certain

Shifts will come

So, now you're focusing more on the parts of what you do that you love

Your Inner Champion (supporting yourself thru cheers and boos)

Admit it

It's gone on long enough

You've been attacking yourself, blowing up mistakes that you make, belittling yourself, stepping back into someone else's shadow

Long enough

Tell your inner critic

The part of your mind that's always bullying you to

Be quiet

Silence the voice without entering into repression so you can hear your inner champion speak

Hear your inner champion shout, "You're a winner!"

"No one can take your place!"

"You were created to soar!"

Admittedly, that's not what the world shows you

Enough knock-downs and it can feel impossible that you were created to soar

Noise from the world drowns out the voice of your inner champion

Quieter and quieter your inner champion becomes

Faster and busier and fuller your life gets

If you're not at the grocery store, you're working in a garden. If you're not working in a garden or at the grocery store, you're sewing new clothes for a friend. If you're not sewing clothes, you're working at the office, pulling an eight to nine-hour day. If you're not working at the office, you're commuting to and from work. If you're not commuting to and from work, you're meeting with your child's teacher. If you're not meeting with your child's teacher, you're cleaning up your home. If you're not cleaning up your home, you're volunteering in the community. If you're not volunteering in the community, you're working on your dream or side gig. If you're not working on your dream, you're working at the worship center that you attend.

And you wonder why you feel tired

And you wonder why you never enter stillness

Long enough

To hear your inner champion remind you that you were created to soar

Life here for you goes on

Not only do you go days, years, without hearing from your inner champion

You get so busy, so hurried, that you forget why you came to this world at all

Disappointments, setbacks, busted dreams, strong headwinds and heartaches leave you feeling that you'd be doing really good if you simply survived

Just survive

You tell yourself

Just endure all the hardships this world brings your way

But something keeps nipping at you

Telling you that you were created for so much more

Much more

So much more

Listen

Can't you hear it?

If you don't hear your inner champion speaking, encouraging you toward greatness, boundless goodness

Sit still

Or maybe get outside and take a walk down a dirt road

The kind of road that takes you back to your root, to your core

And listen

Something within you wants more

Not more things you can sit on a shelf or put in a closet or wear on your body or even see with the human eye

An inner more

More adventure

To watch you tap into your gifts

To be a witness

As you soar!

Chapter 10 – Projecting Your Life

When I first heard about projection, it didn't make sense. On top of that, I was certain that, based on what I had read, I didn't project. Examples I read about projection made it seem like people only project when there's something they want to get rid of, something about themselves, about what they think and feel, they don't want to face.

Then, I heard about projection again and decided to give it more thought. Did I ever hate facing the fact that I did, indeed, engage in mind projection.

According to *Psychology Today*, "Projection is the process of displacing one's feelings onto a different person, animal, or object."[1] Love the projection example *Psychology Today* shares. If someone regularly bullies a person, attacking them for being shy, smart or financially wealthy or poor, the one doing the bullying could hate that very thing about themselves. But being unable to face that inner hatred, they project it outwards onto someone else.

Seemed like something only a coward would do, to me. In A Course In Miracles, I read that it's impossible not to project. What's in the mind extends. There's no way not to do it.

Merriam-Webster describes projection as "the attribution of one's own ideas, feelings, or attitudes to other people or to objects". It's also defined by Merriam-Webster as "the externalization of blame, guilt, or responsibility as a defense against anxiety" and finally projection is described as "the act of throwing or thrusting forward."[2]

It's also impossible not to think. You can become unaware of your thoughts, but that doesn't mean that they are not there. In fact, if you want to know where you're headed, pay attention to your thoughts.

To hear the thoughts in your mind that are below the conscious level, you're going to have to get still. You'll also have to do away with worrying as worrying is a great way to "cover up" what you're truly thinking below the surface.

What's below the surface is what you might be projecting most. Here the wonder of the world rest, in part.

Thoughts you produce work like a cause, making effects that you see "out in" the world. Try it. Change your thoughts about a person, an animal, a song, an experience. Notice how emotions and perceptions (a way of seeing) you have for that person, animal, song or experience change as your thoughts change.

If you have disciplined your mind to recall your dreams by writing your dreams down when you wake, whether you realize it or not, you have witnessed yourself projecting. The only difference between projecting to create dreams and projecting to create daily experiences "out in the world" is that, when you dream at night, you seem to wake up from sleep, thereby more easily accepting that you're the creator of the dreams (inner projection).

Although it takes practice, commitment and, of course, discipline, if you look, you'll see how your perceptions of your experiences are linked to your thoughts. If you're disciplined and you pay attention (practice awareness), you can catch yourself projecting.

References:

1. Projection | Psychology Today
2. Projection Definition & Meaning - Merriam-Webster

What Is Projection?

Thoughts don't stay where they start

They extend, as if poking at something out in the world

Working like roots that demand to shoot up, blossoming into experiences

Pay attention

Hard experiences might be linked to attack thoughts

Doesn't take belief for attack thoughts to start striking out, causing you to move through painful experiences

Try it

Pick one experience to zone in on

Change what you think about the experience

See if emotions tagged to the experience don't alter

Keep shifting your thoughts until your night dreams change

Until the experiences you're having change

You'll be showing yourself --

Clearly showing yourself what projection is

What Do You See Within?

Bright colors leaving flowers, blooming trees, birds and rolling hills in a state of splendor, absolute wonder

Children filling the village with laughter, a welcomed by-product of jumping headlong into play and fun

A couple holding hands, smiling tenderly at one another, their hearts flowing with peace, excitement and happiness for no other reason than that they are together

What do you see when you look within yourself?

Calm that flows like a gentle river?

Volcanic eruptions spewing boiling danger?

What's there . . . when you look within?

Sometimes when I look within, I see bright colors that sparkle and bounce and shine

I see a soothing embrace, signaling that I'm resting in peace, ready to respond with patience to whatever comes my way

Other times, I see battle, one unkind thought after another swirling in my mind, as if seeking a target

Often the target is me

It's as if a part of me doesn't know that, together, we make a whole, we're a part of the same thing

The attacks are brutal, at times leaving me fatigued, too tired to write, exercise, visit a friend or do other activities that I love, activities that open me up to joy and peace

Then, there are the peaceful times

Welcomed experiences when I absolutely love myself

What a joy that is

There is so much to see when I look within

Curious to know if it's the same with you?

Still yourself enough to hear other parts of you speak

See what they have to say

And if you had to draw a picture to illustrate what you see and feel on the inside, what would that picture look like?

Start caring about what you see within

In this world, what you see within is bound to change

But if you know yourself

Truly know yourself

What you see won't shock you

And you'll love yourself

Despite what you see

And you'll change what you know should change, as if you were working on someone else, helping them to be their best self, instead of working to make yourself better

But first you have to look within

There's no reason to fear

As you look within, getting closer to the truth

Closer to your core

You'll only see beauty, the most beautiful, splendid light

Admittedly, it takes work and commitment and consistency to reach your core

Yet you will

And you'll be amazed at what you see

Change Is an Inside Job

Real change requires all of you to participate in

What is about to happen

To invest in what you are about to do

Whether that goal is to fulfill a lifelong dream

Try something new so you can feel invigorated and alive again

Or focus on bringing love alive

That might look like you pursuing becoming more patient, kind,
gracious, forgiving

Either way, regardless of what you choose to make different

It's change

If it's something that you've been thinking about doing for a long
time

Several months, years or even a decade or longer

As painful as working toward a goal for a long time only to remain away from what you want is, there are benefits associated with a long pursuit

Once all of you gets onboard, you're on the path to inner change, the change that incorporates your subconscious into your efforts

Stir your subconscious, your courage and your inner vision and

You could become unstoppable

But first you have to change from the inside

You have to get all of you in on the process

As you do, you'll see and feel different

Welcome these different experiences

These new feelings

Don't push them away, turning away from them in fear

Bid them to come

Changing you more and more

Let them serve as signposts, feelings of excitement, joy, peace and love

Showing you when you're on the right path

Soon you'll learn that when you make decisions that rob you of these emotions

It's a sign that you've ventured off the path

The more you get bogged down with fear, sorrow, hopelessness, despair and fatigue

The more you'll know that you should get still

Remember your core

Feel your core

Wait for guidance

Then step forward

Into new beginnings

With courage, faith, trust and great expectation

Changing more and more

Deeper and deeper

Expanding

Until

The outer world has no choice but to oblige your efforts

Showing you a new, magnificent world

Filled with what you'd been hoping for

Your Thoughts Matter

I was in my middle years when I woke early one morning

Not wanting to get out of bed

Could feel my inner thoughts

They led to a dream that I'm still trying to figure out

Not a bad dream, just a dream that made me curious

Here's the amazing thing

After having experiences in my body for several decades, I was becoming more aware of my thoughts

Becoming more aware of emotions that my thoughts created as well as how my thoughts were guiding me

Almost as if I was telling myself what to do

Intrigue and appreciation flowed within me

I was very curious as to why I hadn't perceived my thoughts this way before

Until this morning, when I felt compelled to do something, I had nearly always felt as if something outside of me was telling me what to do

Now I saw that I was making decisions for myself

Soon I was wondering why I was blocking myself from receiving what I had wanted for more than 20 years

Why wasn't I allowing myself to receive lots more book sales? What thoughts was I incorporating to hold myself back from receiving these book sales?

And why was I blocking myself from receiving the very blessing I may have come into this world to receive?

Rather than to continue to feel angry with myself

I decided to explore the blockage

Which is a process I am committed to regardless of the topic, so I can keep advancing, keep expanding

It's also when I clearly saw how much thoughts matter

If I was telling myself what to do all day and all night

My thoughts had to have been having tremendous impact

Shifting the focus from me to you

What do you tell yourself?

What have you discovered you're telling yourself, whether you caught yourself encouraging, advising or prompting yourself to do something?

Have you noticed how you keep thinking thoughts that generate the same strong emotions?

Maybe you worry about volunteer projects, work, your health (another way to try to figure out how much longer you're going to stay in your body) or a relationship

The thing is, you don't stop worrying until you feel intense confusion, fear, anger, abandonment or perhaps it's an adrenaline rush that you use thoughts to feel

And not just once, but repeatedly

Pay attention to your thoughts

Get still until you become aware of your thoughts

Love yourself throughout this process

Avoid trying to repress or push down thoughts

Simply observe what your mind is doing

See if you can link your thoughts to what's happening in your life, to how you generally feel

Your thoughts matter

The more you become aware of them, the better

Becoming aware of your thoughts keeps things unhidden

Helps to avoid the types of surprises that could leave you stuck, spinning in circles or living with the emotion of fear

Allows you to see that you have the keys and the ability to *choose again* when you find yourself in relationships, jobs and living arrangements that you don't enjoy, relationships that rob you of peace, love and joy

But don't just become aware of your thoughts

Accept responsibility for your thoughts

If you find it hard to believe that a thought is yours (coming from within you)

Continue to explore the thought

You might be surprised to find a belief about something from the past linked to the thought, causing the thought to repeat

Or you might find love or fear pinned to a thought

As you explore thoughts, you can go free of habits, patterns and beliefs that have held you back

Thoughts matter

They matter a lot

Choose thoughts that lead you into peace, love and joy!

Chapter 11 - Waking Up

Waking up is necessary to enter reality. As comfortable as it can feel to stay asleep, it's impossible to experience reality in a sleeping state.

Sweet dreams, happy experiences, can make it easier to wake up. You expect your waking life to be as sweet as the dreams you just released.

On the other hand, if your life feels like a nightmare, waking up could feel scary. As happens with waking from sweet dreams, you might feel as if reality will mirror your sleeping state.

That could make waking frightening. It could also tempt you to resist waking up, believing that to awaken would thrust you into torment or continual heightened fear states.

However you perceive waking up to reality, leaving the dream world behind, if you want to depart the world of illusion, you must awaken. Be gentle with yourself by introducing conflict-free and loving experiences into your life now.

Perceiving Differently

Perception is the vision most used in this world. As you perceive, you assign meanings to what you see, feel and experience. You use perception to understand your environment, yourself and other beings.

Perceiving differently is a way of starting to see differently

To really begin to see what you think and believe

You don't need to feel completely safe to perceive through light

All it takes is a little open mindedness, a little opening to allow light to enter a closed off part of your mind

Maybe you open up to consider that thoughts you have about love, relationships, work or stillness are not entirely accurate

Maybe you allow yourself to start asking the questions you have been wanting real answers to since you were a kid

Step by step

Thought by thought

Belief by belief

Letting go of one hard thought, one seemingly impossible to let go belief after another

Opening up

Going free

Allowing love to chart the course

Swapping fear for love, as simple as that, as easy as snapping your fingers

Just making the exchange

No money or sacrifice required

Just a little willingness to open up

To something new

A path led by and overflowing with love

The path you were always meant to travel

Look again

Perceive anew

Let your life be refreshed

This time and forever

Perceive yourself as an extension of love

Off Brain Auto-Pilot

Turn off the switch

Free yourself of worn out patterns and routines

Take your brain off auto-pilot

Let yourself do something different or allow yourself to do the same thing differently

Get away from living in a repetitive warp

To the tune, rhythm and beat of routine

Boring patterns that have long since birthed fatigue in you, causing you to wonder if the life you're currently living offers sufficient reward for the struggles, the contrast and the challenges you've already faced

It's going to take effort, but not too much

You'll have to focus and live with the blessing of a commitment to practice awareness

Practicing awareness helps you catch yourself thinking and living while your brain is on auto-pilot

Life just repeats

It just repeats and

Repeats and

Repeats

While your brain is on auto-pilot

Your brain on auto-pilot makes the world feel smaller and smaller until you feel trapped by the bounds of repetition

Why stay on auto-pilot when there's so much more to explore, so much more to see and experience?

At best, auto-pilot offers an illusion of safety, comfort, if you will, but it's not real

It's not real safety

Instead it's a binding, a tightening

The act of putting your life in a grip, a smaller space

Want to get out of the grip of routine and repetition?

Do something different, something rooted in love

Observe how you respond to the change

Will you dance?

Will you sing?

Will you play?

Will you laugh?

What will you do while you live off auto-pilot?

Get really creative?

Write the poetry, lyrics, play, script or novel you've dreamed about writing for years?

Dance on stage absent an ounce of fear?

Lead a cause?

Prepare a unique dish that has your personality all over it, then invite everyone you know to feast on the meal?

Run a marathon for the first time?

Climb a mountain?

Build a cabin in the countryside?

Move to a bustling city and make new friends?

Start a business?

What will you do when you come off auto-pilot?

Honest Living

I'm headed for honest living

Going to sink myself fully into living honestly

No more lying to myself

Deceiving myself by telling myself that things are better or worse than they actually are

No more lying about my weight or unhealthy dietary, emotional, psychological, work, relationship or financial habits

You see, the lies, they felt good

Real good, as a matter of fact

When I ate my body fat, I felt sleek and fit

Abusive relationship? No problem, I'd just lie to myself with the assurance that all relationships turn crappy at some point, if they're not always already that way

Keeping the realization of my dreams on hold? Not to worry; I could lie to myself with daydreams, trying to make myself believe that I already had what I was only daydreaming about

It works

My guess is that it would work for as long as I'm in this world

But I would never really have what I truly want

The life I really wanted would always be "out there" somewhere waiting for the real me to show up

That's the worse kind of postponement

Lying postpones good living, puts it off

Then it's all over

Before the "it's all over" arrives for me

I'm changing

Time for honest living

No more just daydreaming, shifting my brain's limbic system, so I'm rewarded emotionally with pleasure even as nothing in my life "really" changes, really moves forward

I really do want what I want, and I'm going after it

The difference this time is that I know to get what I really want, I have to – I must stop lying to myself

Time for honest living

Extending Love

Who knows why love wants to extend itself

It's the strongest impulse

Do you feel your best, happiest, most fulfilled when you operate
from love, when your root is love?

When you're being loving

When you allow yourself to receive and be loved

It's like you've come alive

A rebirth of sorts, not once, but every time it happens

Yet, if love is in everything and is everywhere

Why would love want to extend itself?

There's no place it isn't already

So why extend?

This is a question I have yet to discover the answer for

Why would love, something that is supposed to be everywhere,
the creator of all that is in truth, want to extend itself?

The question becomes part of a riddle that may never be solved

Yet, love calls, almost demands to be shared

To extend

I feel good when I love

I feel good when I let myself be loved

Perhaps love is the most rewarding thing there is

Perhaps love is the most insistent thing there is

It calls and calls and calls

Extending itself wherever reality is

Wherever you are

Your True, Original Self

Keep probing

Searching

Looking and you will see

Your True, original Self

is amazing

Your creation is not an accident

What you really are is needed, so valuable

In this world, you may never understand what you fully are

You know how to love

Does that surprise you?

You're patient

How often have you perceived yourself that way?

Kind

When's the last time you felt your heart open full and ripe with kindness?

Deserving of endless love

Do you blush when people shower you with love, real love – nothing to do with the body?

Able to overcome challenges

One, two, three – How many setbacks have you come through?

Dependable

Just when did you stop seeing yourself this way?

You're so incredible there may be no greater reward than to come home to the One True You

Ending a separation that never should have been

Seeing your Original, True Self clearly

Once

for eternity

Continue the journey

Wisdom knows the way

Wake up

To inner beauty

Wake up

It's not something you have to strive for

It's something you have to accept

Receive that

You're a winner

A champion, not in compliment

It is the truth

Are you starting to remember?

What you were like in your original created state?

Lacking nothing

Free of fear and illusions

A wonder to behold

Love extending itself

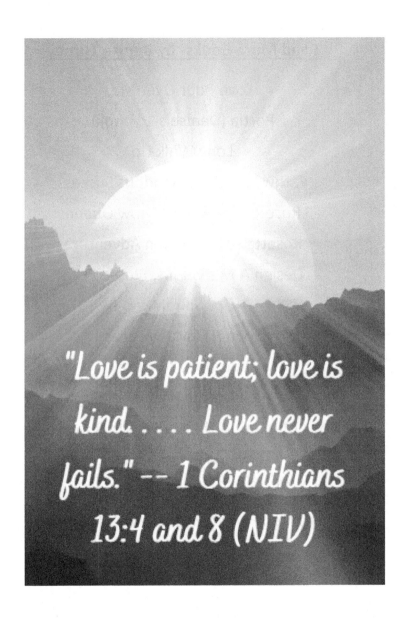

"Love is patient; love is kind. . . . . Love never fails." -- 1 Corinthians 13:4 and 8 (NIV)

Read More Books- by Denise Turney

Love Pour Over Me

Portia (Denise's 1st book)

Long Walk Up

Pathways To Tremendous Success

Rosetta The Talent Show Queen

Rosetta's New Action Adventure

Design A Marvelous, Blessed Life

Spiral

Love Has Many Faces

Your Amazing Life

Awaken Blessings of Inner Love

Book Marketing That Drives Up Book Sales

Love As A Way Of Life

Escaping Toward Freedom

Whooten Forest Mystery: Ties That Bind

Visit Denise Turney online – www.chistell.com

Made in the USA
Las Vegas, NV
23 June 2023

73794985R00075